# Lake Superior

◗ *Indicates Lighthouses Pictured*
● *Not Pictured*

**Lake Superior** is the largest, deepest and also the coldest of the five Great Lakes.

The first lighthouses on the lake were at Whitefish Point and Copper Harbor, both built in 1849. Many others soon followed.

During the mid-1800's, with the discovery of iron ore and copper in Michigan's Upper Peninsula, the need for shipping from Lake Superior became so important that locks were built at Sault Ste. Marie. The locks allow ships to bypass the rapids of the St. Marys River which joins Lake Superior and Lake Huron where the water level is twenty-one feet lower.

Lake Superior has a few islands and lots of irregular rocky shorelines that are hazardous for boaters. In time, most of these places were marked with lights and lighthouses to guide the brave sailors and all those who ventured out on its waters.

*Above: Duluth North Breakwater MN, 1910*
*1. Grand Marais, MN, 1922*
*2. Wisconsin Point (Superior South), WI, 1913*
*3. Duluth South Breakwater Outer, MN, 1901*
*4. Two Harbors, MN, 1892*
*Far Left: Split Rock, MN, 1910*

*Above: Devil's Island, Apostle Islands, WI, 1901*
*1. Keeper's quarters at Devil's Island, Apostle Islands*
*2. Sand Island, WI, 1881*
*3. Outer Island, Apostle Islands, WI, 1874*
*4. Raspberry Island, Apostle Islands, WI, 1863*
*5.  Michigan Island, (Second Light) WI, 1929*
*6. Eagle Harbor, MI, 1871*
*7. Manitou Island, MI, 1861*
*8. Gull Rock , MI, 1867*

1

2

3

4

5

6

*Above: Grand Island East Channel, MI, 1868*
1. *Copper Harbor, MI, 1866*
2. *Marquette Harbor, MI, 1866*
3. *Fourth Order Fresnel Lens at Whitefish Point*
4. *Whitefish Point, MI, 1861*
5. *Crisp Point, MI, 1904*
6. *Point Iroquois, MI, 1871*

# Lake Michigan

**Lake Michigan** first became busy with a variety of ships ranging from small fishing boats, that would venture out in all kinds of weather, to sailing sloops carrying lumber from northern ports to the cities of Chicago and Milwaukee. Great passenger excursion ships traveled to vacation places like Harbor Springs and Mackinac Island. Steel mills at Gary, Indiana brought north-south traffic and railroad car ferries crisscrossed the lake east and west between Michigan and Wisconsin.

Lake Michigan's lighthouses are scattered along the shores of the lake from the great city of Chicago to remote St. Helena Island in the Straits of Mackinac. In the northern region there are a number of lighthouses on offshore islands and simple crib-type foundations that mark shoals out in the lake. Lake Michigan's lights have such a variety of shapes and styles that it is a never-ending pleasure to travel around the lake to see them. In order to view all of them, one would travel through the states of Michigan, Wisconsin, Illinois and Indiana. Most have easy access, but there are a few that can only be reached by boat.

Along the eastern shore the lighthouses at Manistee, Grand Haven, South Haven, St. Joseph and Michigan City all have the original catwalks that were used by the keepers to service the lights during bad weather.

1. *Chicago Harbor, IL, 1893*
2. *Wind Point, WI, 1880*
3. *Pilot Island, WI, 1858*
4. *Sturgeon Bay Ship Canal North Pierhead, WI, 1903*

Above: Peshtigo Reef, WI, 1934

1. Menominee North Pier, MI, 1927
2. Escanaba, MI, 1933
3. Sand Point, MI, 1868
4. Seul Choix, MI, 1895
5. St. Helena, MI, 1873
6. Waugoshance, MI, 1851
7. White Shoal, MI, 1910
8. Beaver Island (St. James Harbor), MI 1870

1

4

2

5

3

6

1. *Skillagalee (Isle Aux Galets), MI, 1888*
2. *Charlevoix South Pier, MI, 1948*
3. *Little Traverse, MI, 1884*
4. *Mission Point (Old Mission Point), MI, 1870*
5. *Point Betsie, MI, 1858*
6. *South Manitou Island, MI 1872*
7. *Grand Traverse, MI, 1858*
8. *Manning Memorial, MI, 1991*

Above: Big Sable Point, MI, 1867
1. Manistee North Pierhead, MI, 1927
2. Grand Haven South Pier, MI, inner 1905, outer 1875
3. Little Sable, MI 1874
4. Holland Harbor, MI, 1907
5. St. Joseph North Pier, MI, 1907
6. Michigan City East Pier, IN, 1904
Following Page: South Haven South Pier, MI 1903

4

5

6

# Lake Huron

**Lake Huron** is located in the middle of the five Great Lakes. Voyageurs in canoes laden with furs and supplies traveled Lake Huron some three hundred years ago. It was a time when Mackinac Island became a trading post and furs were shipped from the lakes to markets in Europe. Now ships from world ports traveling through the St. Lawrence Seaway pass through Lake Huron to ports in Chicago and Duluth. Bulk carriers bring iron ore from Minnesota and Northern Michigan through the lake to ports in Ohio.

Lighthouses are located along the shore from Port Huron to Cheboygan and into the Straits of Mackinac. In the northern region many lights are offshore like the classic Round Island Lighthouse that greets visitors entering the Mackinac Island Harbor. The De Tour Reef Light guides ships passing into the St. Marys River waterway heading toward the Soo Locks and Lake Superior. The Lightship Huron, the only lightship on the Great Lakes, is open to the public at Port Huron where the waters of Lake Huron flow into the St. Clair River on the way to Lake Erie.

1. *Round Island, MI, 1896*
2. *Round Island before restoration*
3. *De Tour Reef, MI, 1931*
4. *Spectacle Reef, MI, 1874*
5. *Old Mackinac Point, MI, 1892*

2

3

4

5

1. Cheboygan Crib, MI, 1884
2. Fourteen Foot Shoal, MI, 1930
3. Poe Reef, MI, 1929
4. Forty Mile Point, MI, 1896
5. Alpena, MI 1914
6. Old Presque Isle, MI, 1840
7. Third Order Fresnel Lens
8. Sturgeon Point, MI, 1870
9. Tawas Point, MI, 1876
Far Right: Presque Isle, MI, 1870

6

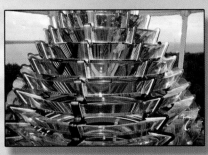

7

8

9

Far Left: Pointe Aux Barques MI, 1876

1. Port Sanilac, MI, 1886
2. Fort Gratiot, MI, 1829
3. Lightship Huron, MI, 1935
4. Ship's Wheel
5. Ship's Lens
6. Ship's Tower
7. William Livingstone Memorial, MI, 1929
8. Peche Island, Marine City, MI, 1908

# Lake Erie

**Lake Erie** stretches from Detroit and Toledo in the west to Buffalo and Niagara Falls in the east. It borders on the states of Michigan, Ohio, Pennsylvania and New York in the United States and Ontario in Canada to the north. In the past, large passenger steamers plied the waters between Detroit, Toledo, Cleveland and Buffalo. Now many bulk carriers including the thousand-foot super ships shuttle iron ore and coal back and forth across the length of the lake. Commercial fishing was important until the blue pike became extinct from over-fishing. Now recreational and sport fishing are more popular than ever with consistently good catches of walleye and lake perch.

Lighthouses have played an important role in the transportation business on Lake Erie. Most lighthouses mark harbor entrances and can be visited while touring the shoreline. Museums of special lighthouse and marine interests are located at Marblehead, Vermilion (Grand River), Old Fairport Main and Ashtabula in Ohio and there is an interesting museum at the Dunkirk Light Station in Dunkirk, New York.

*Top: Marblehead, OH, 1821*
*Lower: South Bass Island, OH, 1897*
*Facing Page: Marblehead at Dawn*

1. Huron Harbor, OH, 1936
2. Lorain West Breakwater, OH, 1917
3. Vermilion, OH, 1991
4. Cleveland West Breakwater, OH, 1911
5. Fairport Harbor West, OH, 1925
6. Old Fairport Main (Grand River), OH, 1871
Far Right: Ashtabula Harbor 1916

1

2

Far Left: Erie Land, PA, 1867
1. Conneaut, OH, 1835
2. Barcelona, NY, 1829
3. Dunkirk, NY, 1875
4. Third Order Fresnel Lens at Dunkirk
5. Bottle Light at Buffalo, NY, 1903
6. Buffalo Main, NY, 1833

# Lake Ontario

**Lake Ontario** is the smallest of the Great Lakes. Water flows from Lake Erie over the Niagara escarpment at the spectacular Niagara Falls before entering Lake Ontario. Ocean-going saltwater ships from world ports must travel through the St. Lawrence Seaway, the length of Lake Ontario and around Niagara Falls by way of the Locks of the Welland Canal. Because of the size of the Welland Canal Locks, the thirteen one thousand foot long super ships that carry iron ore are forever destined to stay above Niagara Falls and Lake Ontario.

Lighthouses mark the various harbors and hazards along the shore and are relatively easy to see along New York's scenic Lake Ontario shoreline. Museums and special places are at Fort Niagara, Thirty Mile Point, Charlotte-Genesee at Rochester, Old Sodus Point, Selkirk and Tibbetts Point at Cape Vincent.

*Right: Fort Niagara, NY 1872*
*1. Thirty Mile Point, NY, 1875*
*2. Charlotte-Genesee, NY, 1822*
*3. Old Sodus Point, NY, 1871*
*4. Oswego, NY, 1934*

1

2

3

4

*Above: Tibbetts Point, NY, 1854*
*1. Selkirk, NY, 1838*
*2. Stony Point, NY, 1869*
*3. Cape Vincent, NY, 1900*